CELEBRATE A YEAR OF POSSIBILITIES!

This planner belongs to

_____

School _____

Grade _____ Room _____

Address _____

_____

Phone _____

Contacts and Volunteers

Name	Contact Info

WELCOME

Schedule

School Begins: _____
Lunch: _____ Recess: _____
Specials: _____
_____
School Ends: _____

Need Help?

Reliable Students: _____
Teachers: _____
Principal: _____
Vice Principal: _____
Other Staff: _____

Special Schedules

Name	Time/Location
_____	_____
_____	_____
_____	_____
_____	_____

Additional Notes

_____
_____
_____
_____
_____

Communication Log

Date	Type	Name	Purpose	Notes
	📱 @ 📄 👥			
	📱 @ 📄 👥			
	📱 @ 📄 👥			
	📱 @ 📄 👥			
	📱 @ 📄 👥			
	📱 @ 📄 👥			
	📱 @ 📄 👥			
	📱 @ 📄 👥			
	📱 @ 📄 👥			
	📱 @ 📄 👥			
	📱 @ 📄 👥			
	📱 @ 📄 👥			
	📱 @ 📄 👥			
	📱 @ 📄 👥			
	📱 @ 📄 👥			
	📱 @ 📄 👥			
	📱 @ 📄 👥			
	📱 @ 📄 👥			
	📱 @ 📄 👥			
	📱 @ 📄 👥			
	📱 @ 📄 👥			
	📱 @ 📄 👥			
	📱 @ 📄 👥			
	📱 @ 📄 👥			
	📱 @ 📄 👥			
	📱 @ 📄 👥			
	📱 @ 📄 👥			

Communication Log

Date	Type	Name	Purpose	Notes
	📱 @ 📄 👥			
	📱 @ 📄 👥			
	📱 @ 📄 👥			
	📱 @ 📄 👥			
	📱 @ 📄 👥			
	📱 @ 📄 👥			
	📱 @ 📄 👥			
	📱 @ 📄 👥			
	📱 @ 📄 👥			
	📱 @ 📄 👥			
	📱 @ 📄 👥			
	📱 @ 📄 👥			
	📱 @ 📄 👥			
	📱 @ 📄 👥			
	📱 @ 📄 👥			
	📱 @ 📄 👥			
	📱 @ 📄 👥			
	📱 @ 📄 👥			
	📱 @ 📄 👥			
	📱 @ 📄 👥			
	📱 @ 📄 👥			
	📱 @ 📄 👥			
	📱 @ 📄 👥			
	📱 @ 📄 👥			
	📱 @ 📄 👥			
	📱 @ 📄 👥			

PLAN IT

Use these pages to create a classroom plan, record seating charts, create checklists, sketch plans, etc. The options are endless!

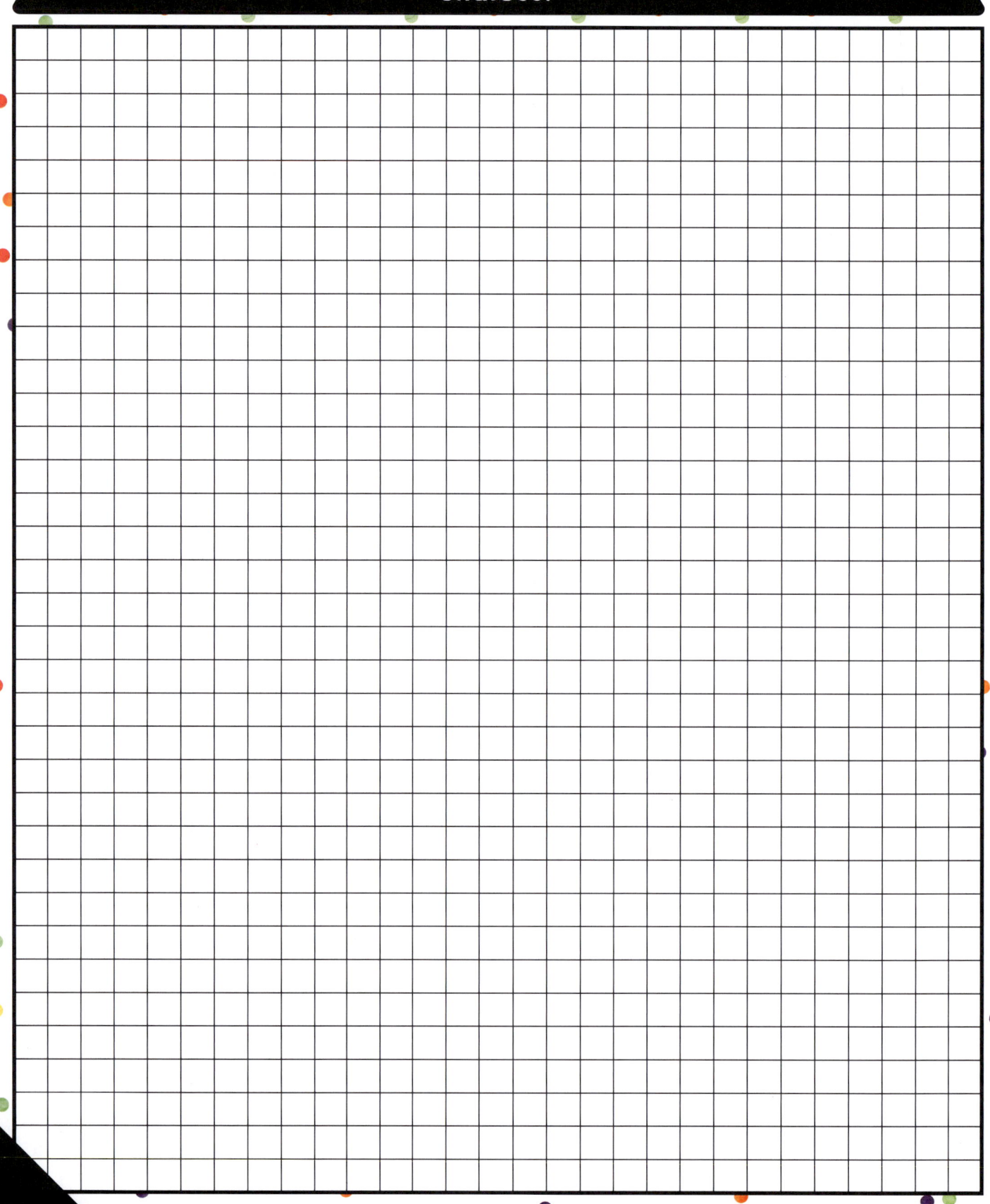

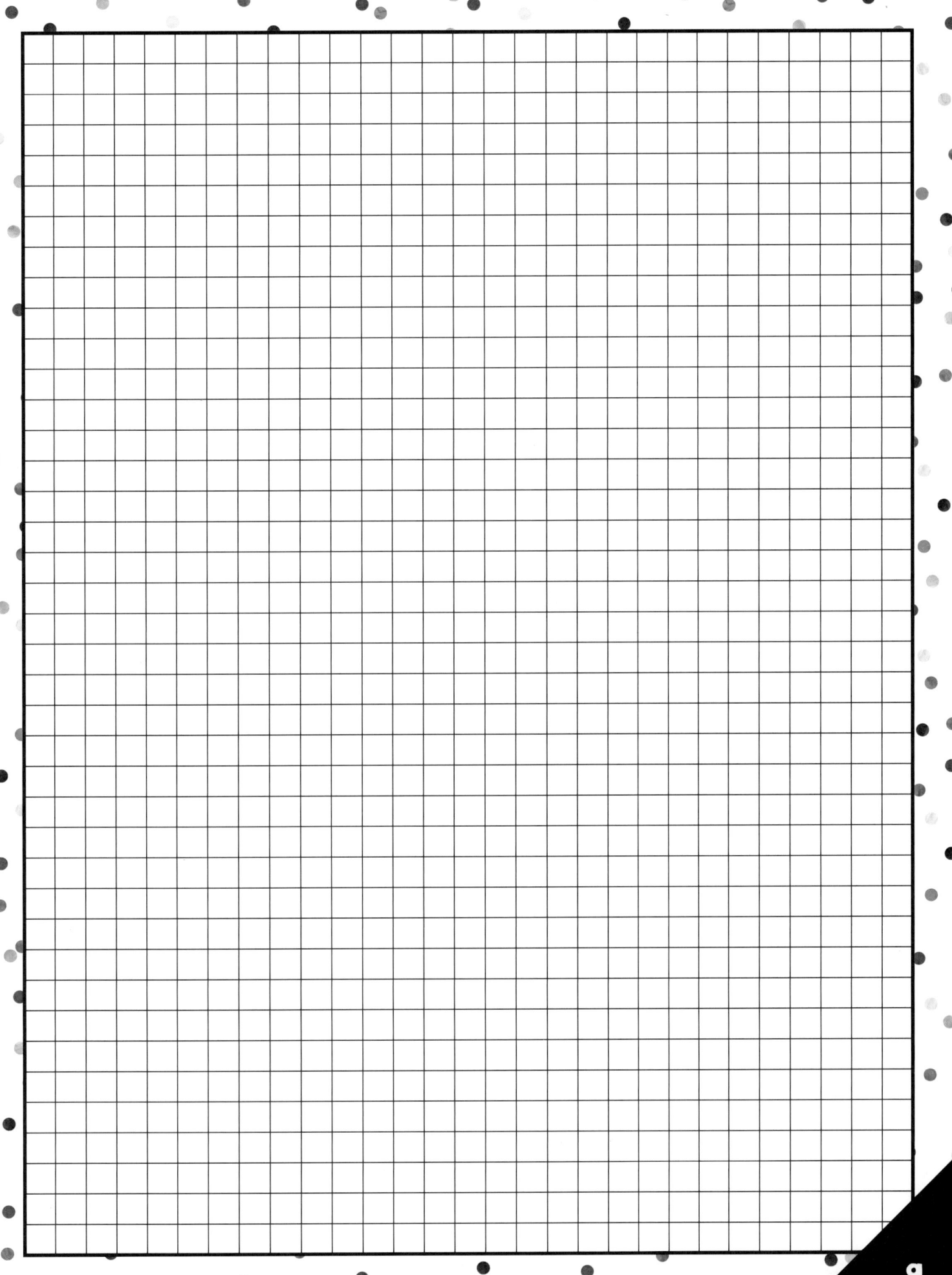

Year @ a Glance

July

August

September

October

November

December

Year @ a Glance

January	February

March	April

May	June

JULY

BE HAPPY, BE BRIGHT, BE YOU!

Sunday	Monday	Tuesday	Wednesday

IMPORTANT DATES		GOALS	

Thursday	Friday	Saturday	HAVE TO DO
			NOTES

PSST! USE THESE GUIDES TO KEEP YOUR TABS PERFECTLY PLACED.

13

AUGUST

CHANGE THE WORLD ONE CHILD AT A TIME.

Sunday	Monday	Tuesday	Wednesday

IMPORTANT DATES

GOALS

Thursday	Friday	Saturday	HAVE TO DO
			○
			○
			○
			○
			○
			○
			○
			NOTES

15

SEPTEMBER

SPARKLE WHERE YOU STAND!

Sunday	Monday	Tuesday	Wednesday

IMPORTANT DATES

GOALS

Thursday	Friday	Saturday	HAVE TO DO
			NOTES

17

OCTOBER

WITHOUT TEACHERS, LIFE WOULD HAVE NO CLASS.

Sunday	Monday	Tuesday	Wednesday

IMPORTANT DATES

GOALS

Thursday	Friday	Saturday	HAVE TO DO

NOTES

19

NOVEMBER

YOU ARE CAPABLE OF AMAZING THINGS.

Sunday	Monday	Tuesday	Wednesday

IMPORTANT DATES

GOALS

Thursday	Friday	Saturday	HAVE TO DO
			○
			○
			○
			○
			NOTES

21

DECEMBER

BIG HEARTS SHAPE LITTLE MINDS.

Sunday	Monday	Tuesday	Wednesday

IMPORTANT DATES

GOALS

Thursday	Friday	Saturday	**HAVE TO DO**

NOTES

23

JANUARY

SAY YES TO SOMETHING NEW!

Sunday	Monday	Tuesday	Wednesday

IMPORTANT DATES

GOALS

Thursday	Friday	Saturday	HAVE TO DO
			NOTES

25

FEBRUARY

THE FUTURE OF THE WORLD IS IN YOUR CLASSROOM.

Sunday	Monday	Tuesday	Wednesday

IMPORTANT DATES

GOALS

Thursday	Friday	Saturday	HAVE TO DO
			NOTES

27

MARCH

STRIVE FOR PROGRESS, NOT PERFECTION.

Sunday	Monday	Tuesday	Wednesday

IMPORTANT DATES
_____
_____
_____
_____

GOALS
_____
_____
_____
_____

Thursday	Friday	Saturday	HAVE TO DO
			○ _____ ○ _____ ○ _____ ○ _____ ○ _____ ○ _____ ○ _____
			○ _____ ○ _____ ○ _____ ○ _____ ○ _____
			NOTES

29

APRIL

THE BEST IS YET TO COME!

Sunday	Monday	Tuesday	Wednesday

IMPORTANT DATES

GOALS

Thursday	Friday	Saturday	HAVE TO DO
			○
			○
			○
			○
			○
			○
			○
			○
			○
			○
			○
			NOTES

31

MAY

ONE KIND WORD CAN CHANGE THE DAY.

Sunday	Monday	Tuesday	Wednesday

IMPORTANT DATES

GOALS

Thursday	Friday	Saturday	HAVE TO DO

NOTES

JUNE

THE BEST PART OF TEACHING IS THAT IT MATTERS.

Sunday	Monday	Tuesday	Wednesday

IMPORTANT DATES

GOALS

Thursday	Friday	Saturday	HAVE TO DO

NOTES

35

WEEK #	SUBJECT	SUBJECT	SUBJECT
MON /			
TUE /			
WED /			
THURS /			
FRI /			

SUBJECT	SUBJECT	SUBJECT	SUBJECT

PSST! CUT THIS CORNER OFF EACH WEEK TO MARK AND FIND YOUR PLACE EASILY

WEEK #	SUBJECT	SUBJECT	SUBJECT
MON /			
TUE /			
WED /			
THURS /			
FRI /			

SUBJECT	SUBJECT	SUBJECT	SUBJECT

WEEK #	SUBJECT	SUBJECT	SUBJECT
MON /			
TUE /			
WED /			
THURS /			
FRI /			

SUBJECT	SUBJECT	SUBJECT	SUBJECT

WEEK #	SUBJECT	SUBJECT	SUBJECT
MON /			
TUE /			
WED /			
THURS /			
FRI /			

SUBJECT	SUBJECT	SUBJECT	SUBJECT

WEEK #	SUBJECT	SUBJECT	SUBJECT
MON /			
TUE /			
WED /			
THURS /			
FRI /			

SUBJECT	SUBJECT	SUBJECT	SUBJECT

WEEK #	SUBJECT	SUBJECT	SUBJECT
MON /			
TUE /			
WED /			
THURS /			
FRI /			

SUBJECT	SUBJECT	SUBJECT	SUBJECT

WEEK #	SUBJECT	SUBJECT	SUBJECT
MON /			
TUE /			
WED /			
THURS /			
FRI /			

SUBJECT	SUBJECT	SUBJECT	SUBJECT

WEEK #	SUBJECT	SUBJECT	SUBJECT
MON /			
TUE /			
WED /			
THURS /			
FRI /			

SUBJECT	SUBJECT	SUBJECT	SUBJECT

	SUBJECT	SUBJECT	SUBJECT
WEEK #			
MON /			
TUE /			
WED /			
THURS /			
FRI /			

SUBJECT	SUBJECT	SUBJECT	SUBJECT

WEEK #	SUBJECT	SUBJECT	SUBJECT
MON /			
TUE /			
WED /			
THURS /			
FRI /			

SUBJECT	SUBJECT	SUBJECT	SUBJECT

WEEK #	SUBJECT	SUBJECT	SUBJECT
MON /			
TUE /			
WED /			
THURS /			
FRI /			

SUBJECT	SUBJECT	SUBJECT	SUBJECT

WEEK #	SUBJECT	SUBJECT	SUBJECT
MON /			
TUE /			
WED /			
THURS /			
FRI /			

SUBJECT	SUBJECT	SUBJECT	SUBJECT

WEEK #	SUBJECT	SUBJECT	SUBJECT
MON /			
TUE /			
WED /			
THURS /			
FRI /			

SUBJECT	SUBJECT	SUBJECT	SUBJECT

WEEK #	SUBJECT	SUBJECT	SUBJECT
MON /			
TUE /			
WED /			
THURS /			
FRI /			

SUBJECT	SUBJECT	SUBJECT	SUBJECT

WEEK #	SUBJECT	SUBJECT	SUBJECT
MON /			
TUE /			
WED /			
THURS /			
FRI /			

SUBJECT	SUBJECT	SUBJECT	SUBJECT

WEEK #	SUBJECT	SUBJECT	SUBJECT
MON /			
TUE /			
WED /			
THURS /			
FRI /			

SUBJECT	SUBJECT	SUBJECT	SUBJECT

WEEK #	SUBJECT	SUBJECT	SUBJECT
MON /			
TUE /			
WED /			
THURS /			
FRI /			

SUBJECT	SUBJECT	SUBJECT	SUBJECT

WEEK #	SUBJECT	SUBJECT	SUBJECT
MON /			
TUE /			
WED /			
THURS /			
FRI /			

SUBJECT	SUBJECT	SUBJECT	SUBJECT

	SUBJECT	SUBJECT	SUBJECT
MON /			
TUE /			
WED /			
THURS /			
FRI /			

WEEK #

SUBJECT	SUBJECT	SUBJECT	SUBJECT

WEEK #	SUBJECT	SUBJECT	SUBJECT
MON /			
TUE /			
WED /			
THURS /			
FRI /			

SUBJECT	SUBJECT	SUBJECT	SUBJECT

WEEK #	SUBJECT	SUBJECT	SUBJECT
MON /			
TUE /			
WED /			
THURS /			
FRI /			

SUBJECT	SUBJECT	SUBJECT	SUBJECT

WEEK #	SUBJECT	SUBJECT	SUBJECT
MON /			
TUE /			
WED /			
THURS /			
FRI /			

SUBJECT	SUBJECT	SUBJECT	SUBJECT

WEEK #	SUBJECT	SUBJECT	SUBJECT
MON /			
TUE /			
WED /			
THURS /			
FRI /			

SUBJECT	SUBJECT	SUBJECT	SUBJECT

WEEK #	SUBJECT	SUBJECT	SUBJECT
MON /			
TUE /			
WED /			
THURS /			
FRI /			

SUBJECT	SUBJECT	SUBJECT	SUBJECT

WEEK #	SUBJECT	SUBJECT	SUBJECT
MON /			
TUE /			
WED /			
THURS /			
FRI /			

SUBJECT	SUBJECT	SUBJECT	SUBJECT

WEEK #	SUBJECT	SUBJECT	SUBJECT
MON /			
TUE /			
WED /			
THURS /			
FRI /			

SUBJECT	SUBJECT	SUBJECT	SUBJECT

WEEK #	SUBJECT	SUBJECT	SUBJECT
MON /			
TUE /			
WED /			
THURS /			
FRI /			

SUBJECT	SUBJECT	SUBJECT	SUBJECT

WEEK #	SUBJECT	SUBJECT	SUBJECT
MON /			
TUE /			
WED /			
THURS /			
FRI /			

SUBJECT	SUBJECT	SUBJECT	SUBJECT

WEEK #	SUBJECT	SUBJECT	SUBJECT
MON /			
TUE /			
WED /			
THURS /			
FRI /			

SUBJECT	SUBJECT	SUBJECT	SUBJECT

WEEK #	SUBJECT	SUBJECT	SUBJECT
MON /			
TUE /			
WED /			
THURS /			
FRI /			

SUBJECT	SUBJECT	SUBJECT	SUBJECT

WEEK #	SUBJECT	SUBJECT	SUBJECT
MON /			
TUE /			
WED /			
THURS /			
FRI /			

SUBJECT	SUBJECT	SUBJECT	SUBJECT

WEEK #	SUBJECT	SUBJECT	SUBJECT
MON /			
TUE /			
WED /			
THURS /			
FRI /			

SUBJECT	SUBJECT	SUBJECT	SUBJECT

WEEK #	SUBJECT	SUBJECT	SUBJECT
MON /			
TUE /			
WED /			
THURS /			
FRI /			

SUBJECT	SUBJECT	SUBJECT	SUBJECT

WEEK #	SUBJECT	SUBJECT	SUBJECT
MON /			
TUE /			
WED /			
THURS /			
FRI /			

SUBJECT	SUBJECT	SUBJECT	SUBJECT

	SUBJECT	SUBJECT	SUBJECT
WEEK #			
MON /			
TUE /			
WED /			
THURS /			
FRI /			

SUBJECT	SUBJECT	SUBJECT	SUBJECT

WEEK #	SUBJECT	SUBJECT	SUBJECT
MON /			
TUE /			
WED /			
THURS /			
FRI /			

SUBJECT	SUBJECT	SUBJECT	SUBJECT

WEEK #	SUBJECT	SUBJECT	SUBJECT
MON /			
TUE /			
WED /			
THURS /			
FRI /			

SUBJECT	SUBJECT	SUBJECT	SUBJECT

WEEK #	SUBJECT	SUBJECT	SUBJECT
MON /			
TUE /			
WED /			
THURS /			
FRI /			

SUBJECT	SUBJECT	SUBJECT	SUBJECT

WEEK #	SUBJECT	SUBJECT	SUBJECT
MON /			
TUE /			
WED /			
THURS /			
FRI /			

SUBJECT	SUBJECT	SUBJECT	SUBJECT

WEEK #	SUBJECT	SUBJECT	SUBJECT
MON /			
TUE /			
WED /			
THURS /			
FRI /			

SUBJECT	SUBJECT	SUBJECT	SUBJECT

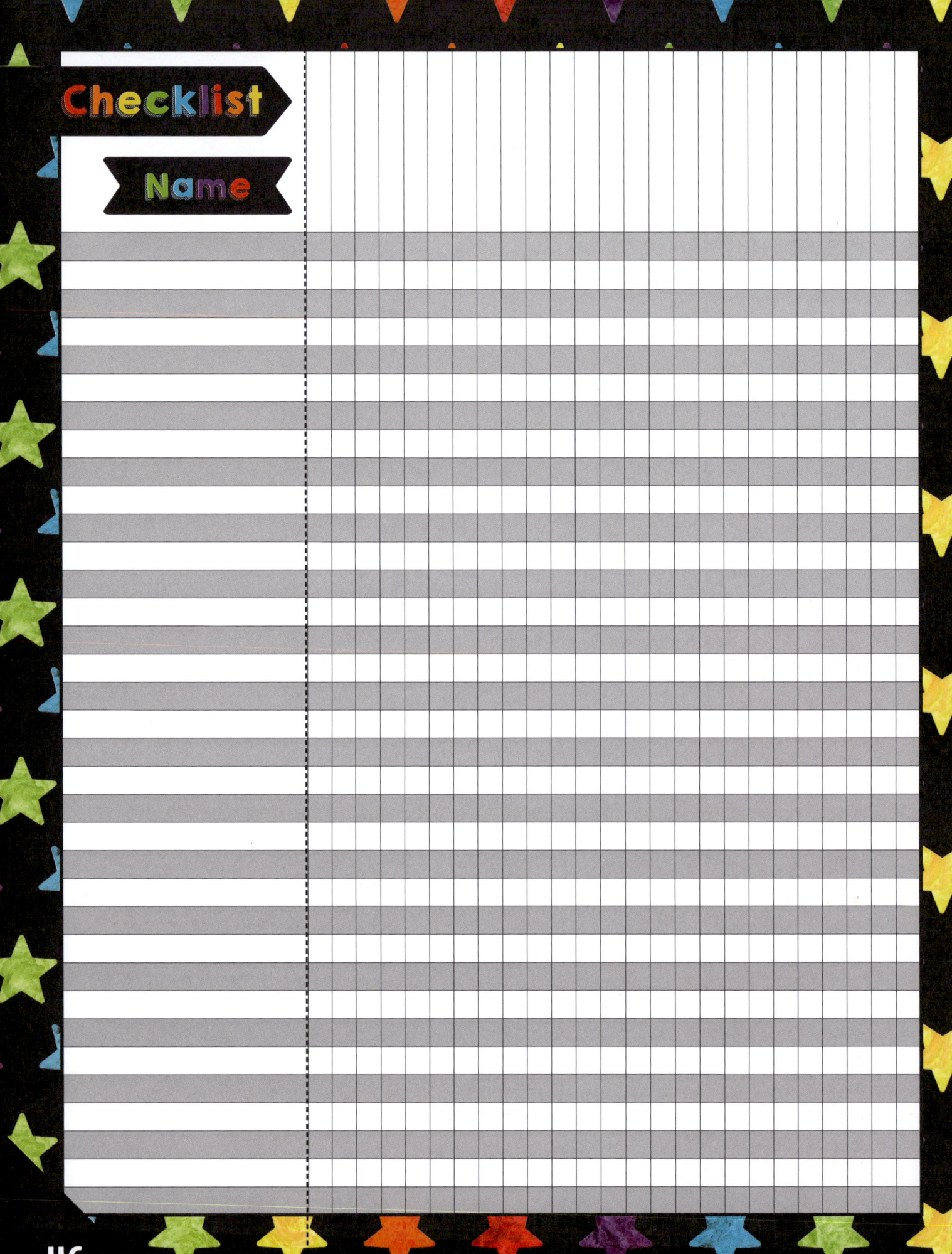

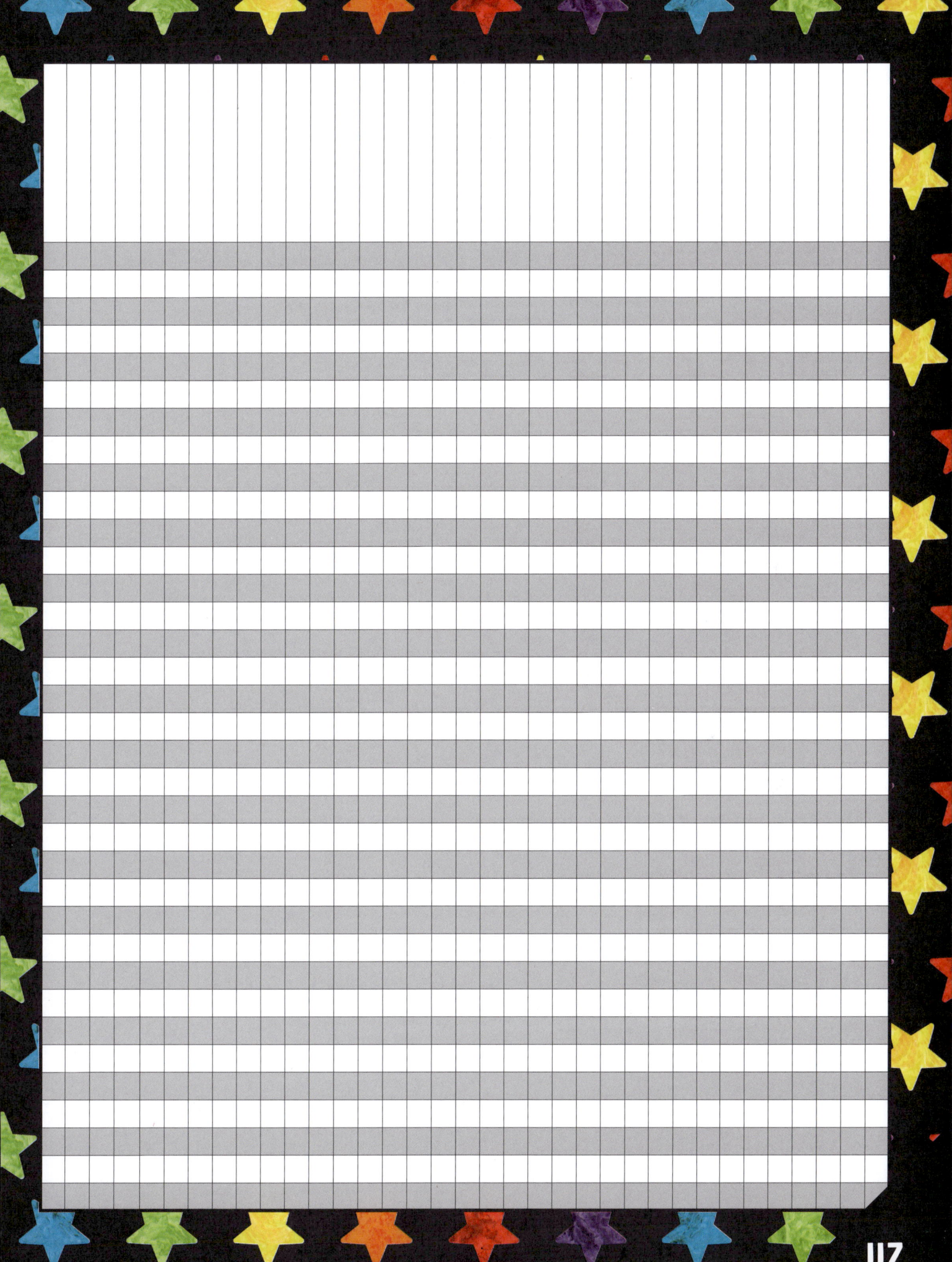

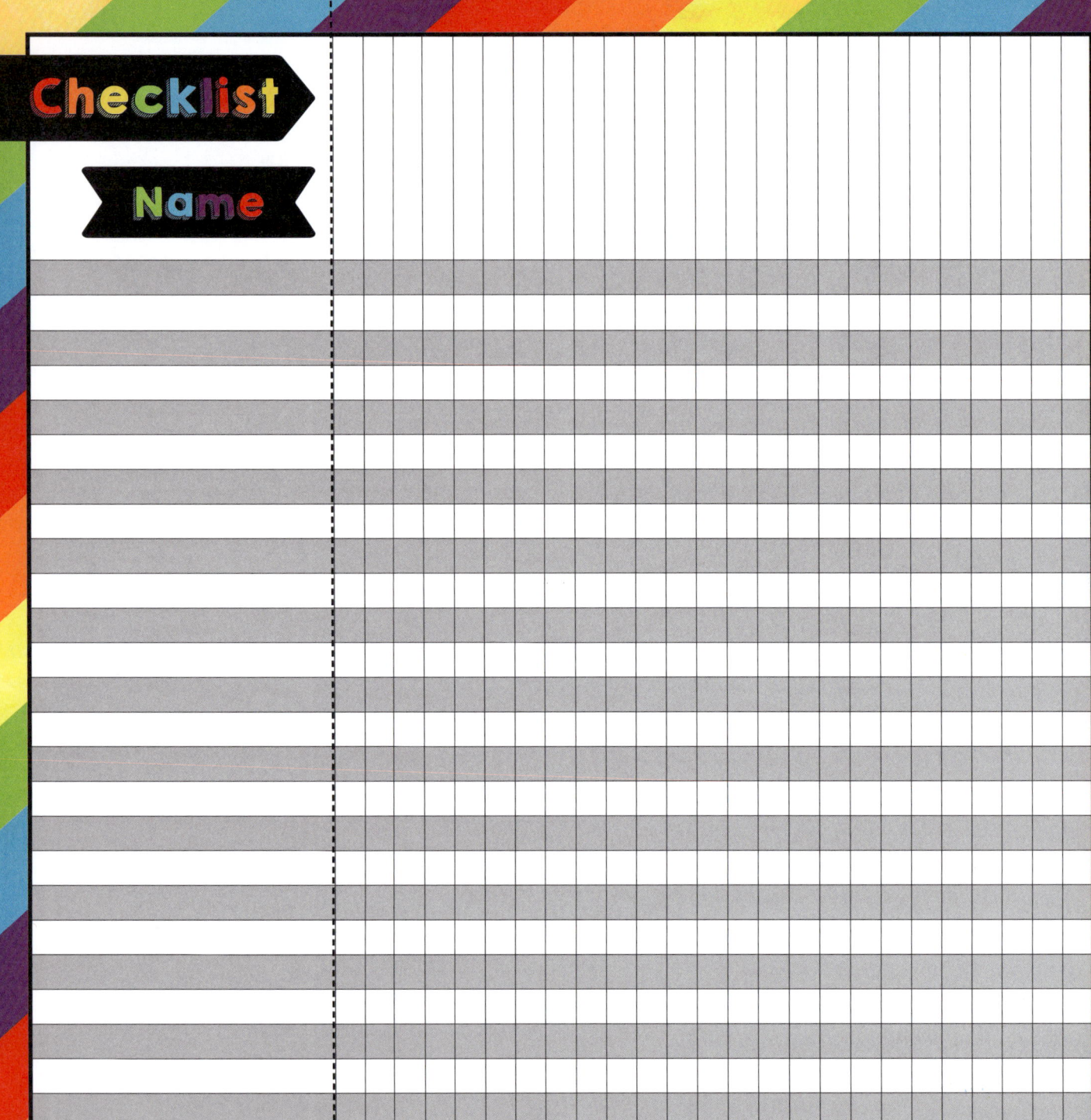

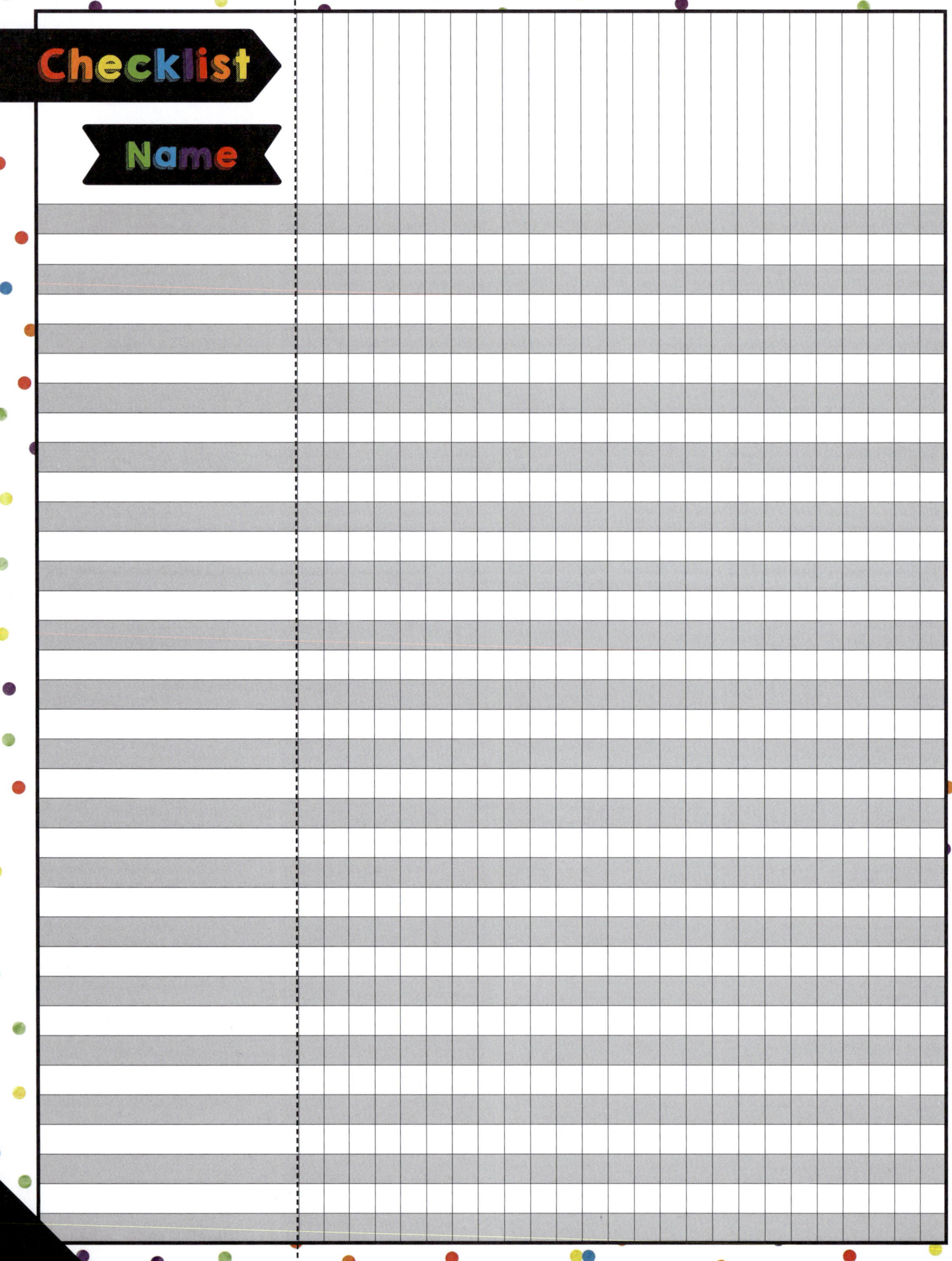

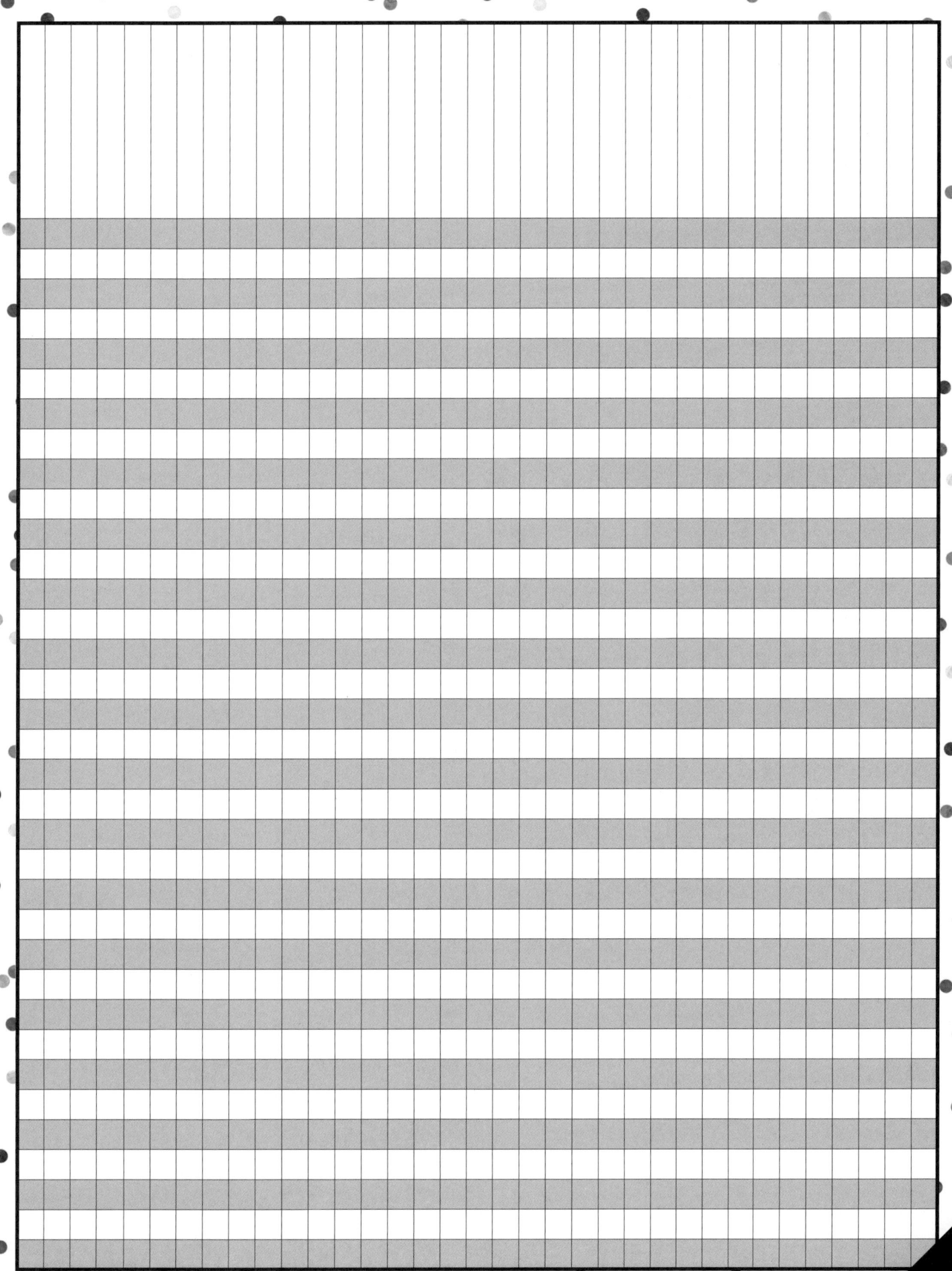

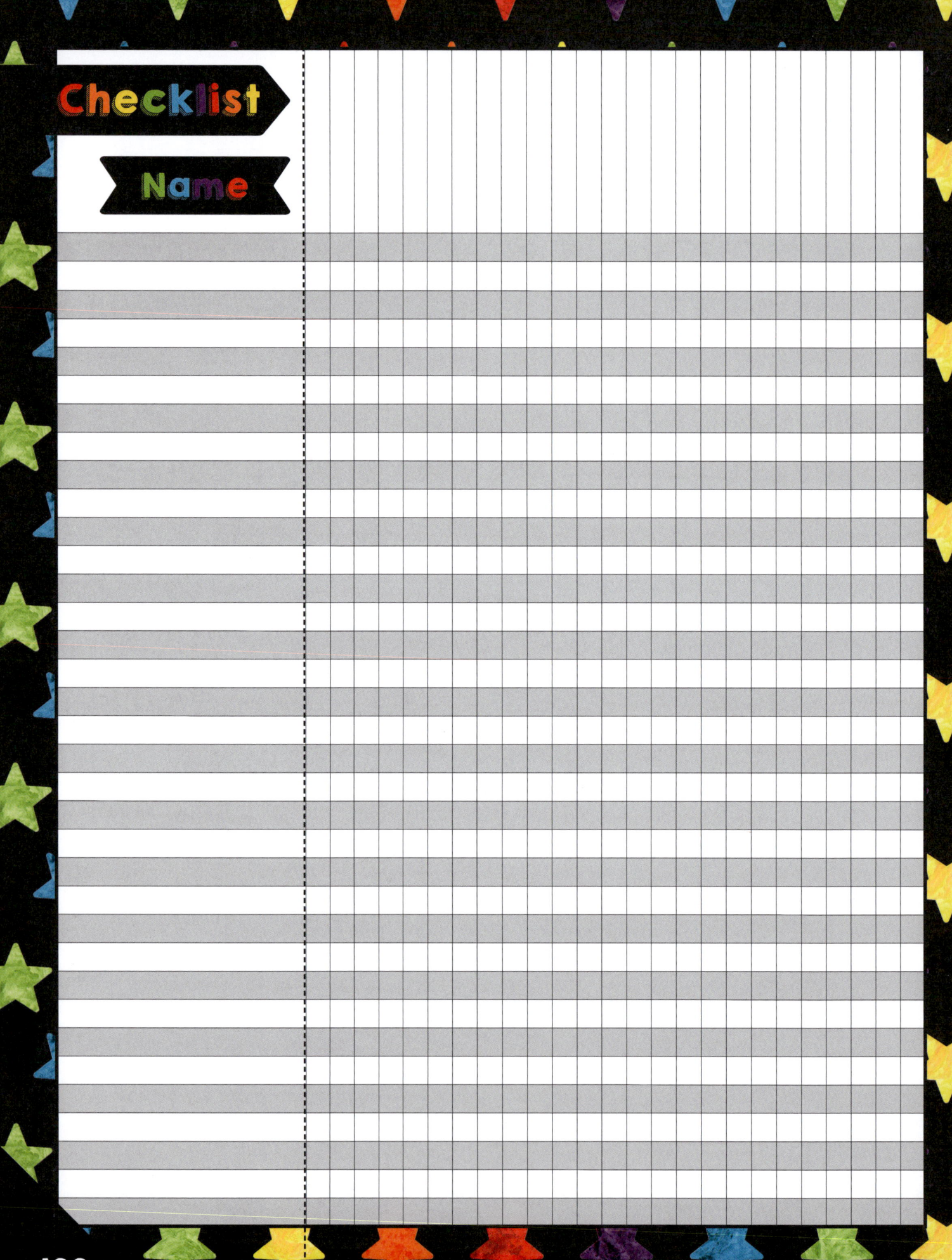

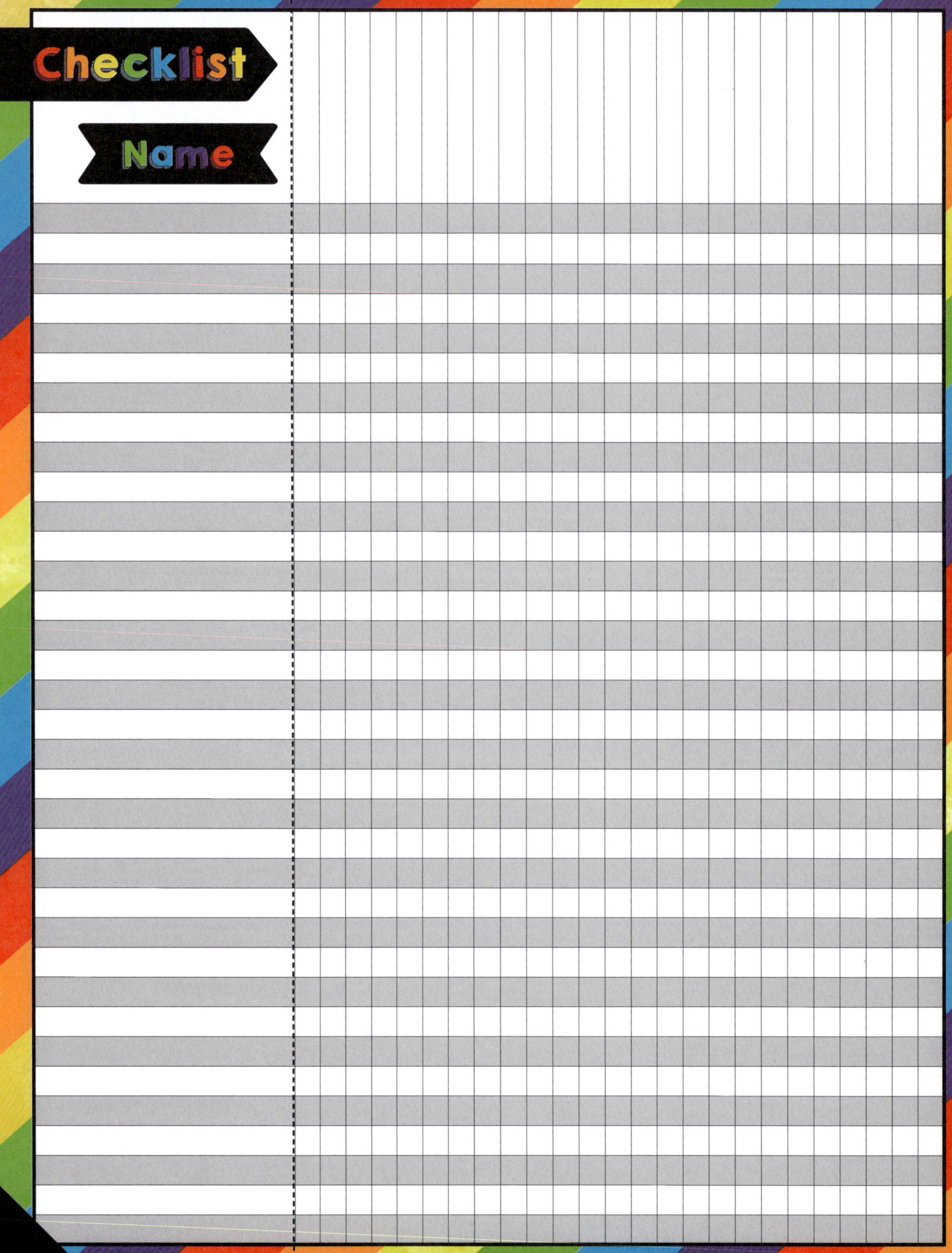

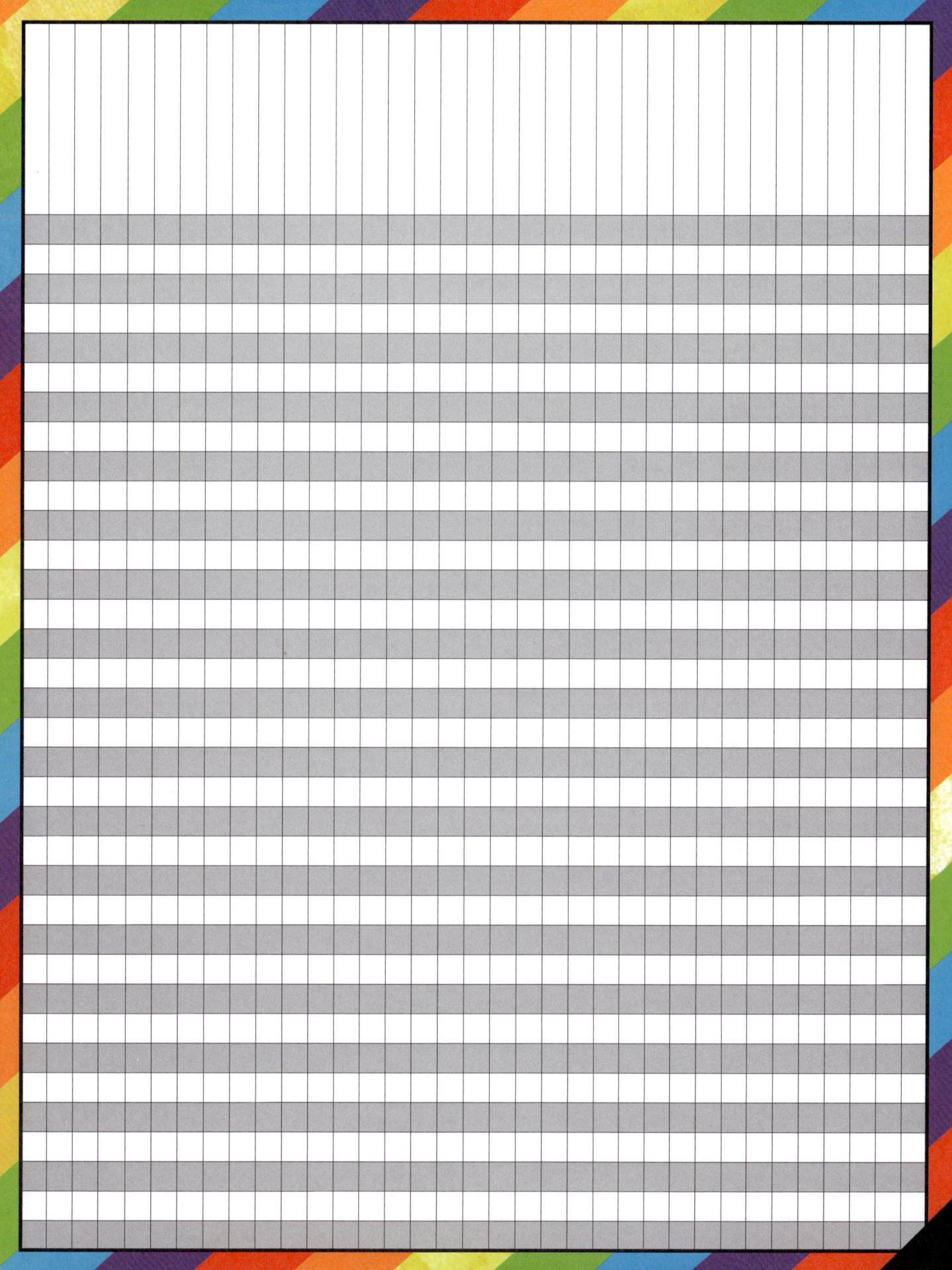

Checklist

Name

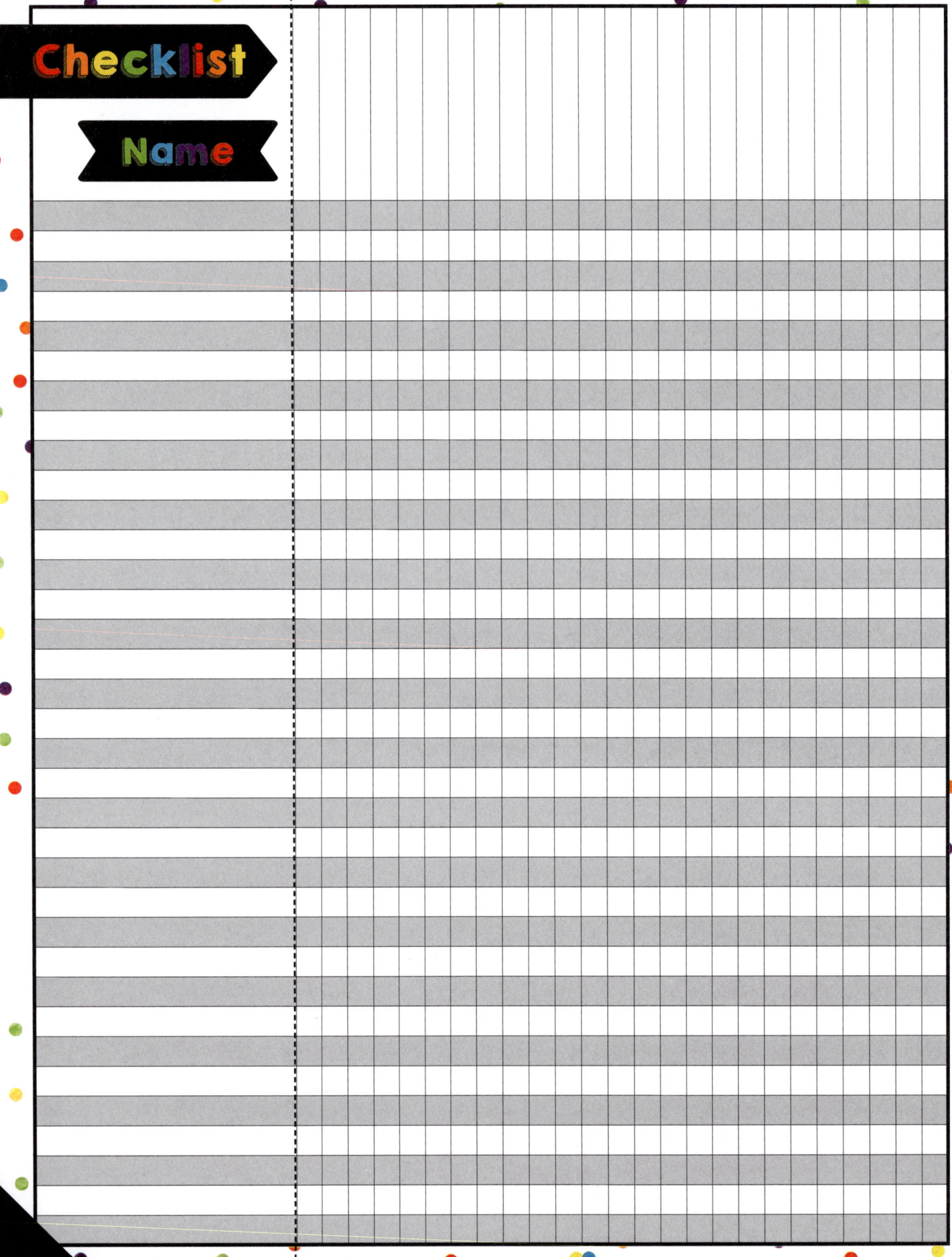

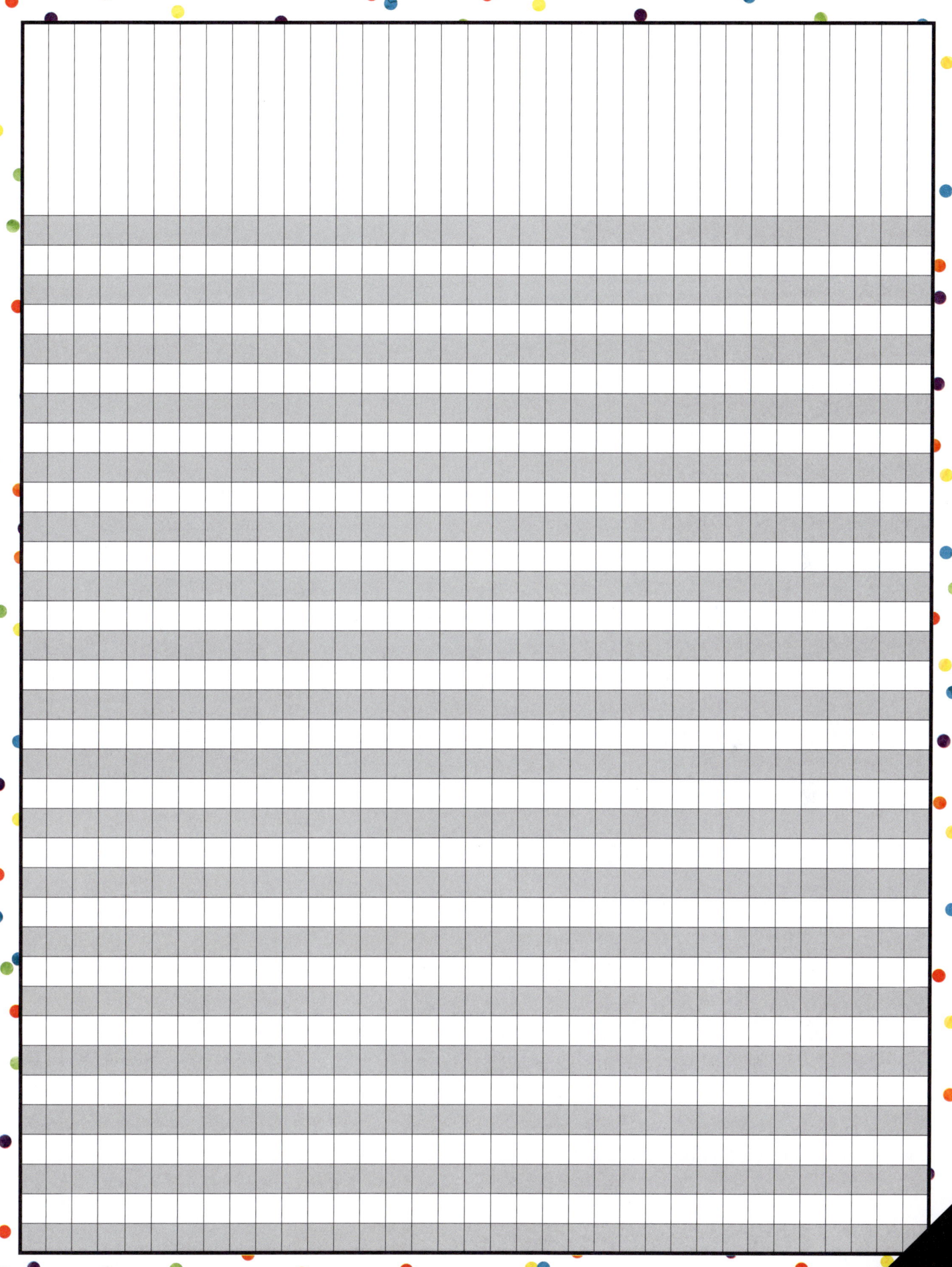

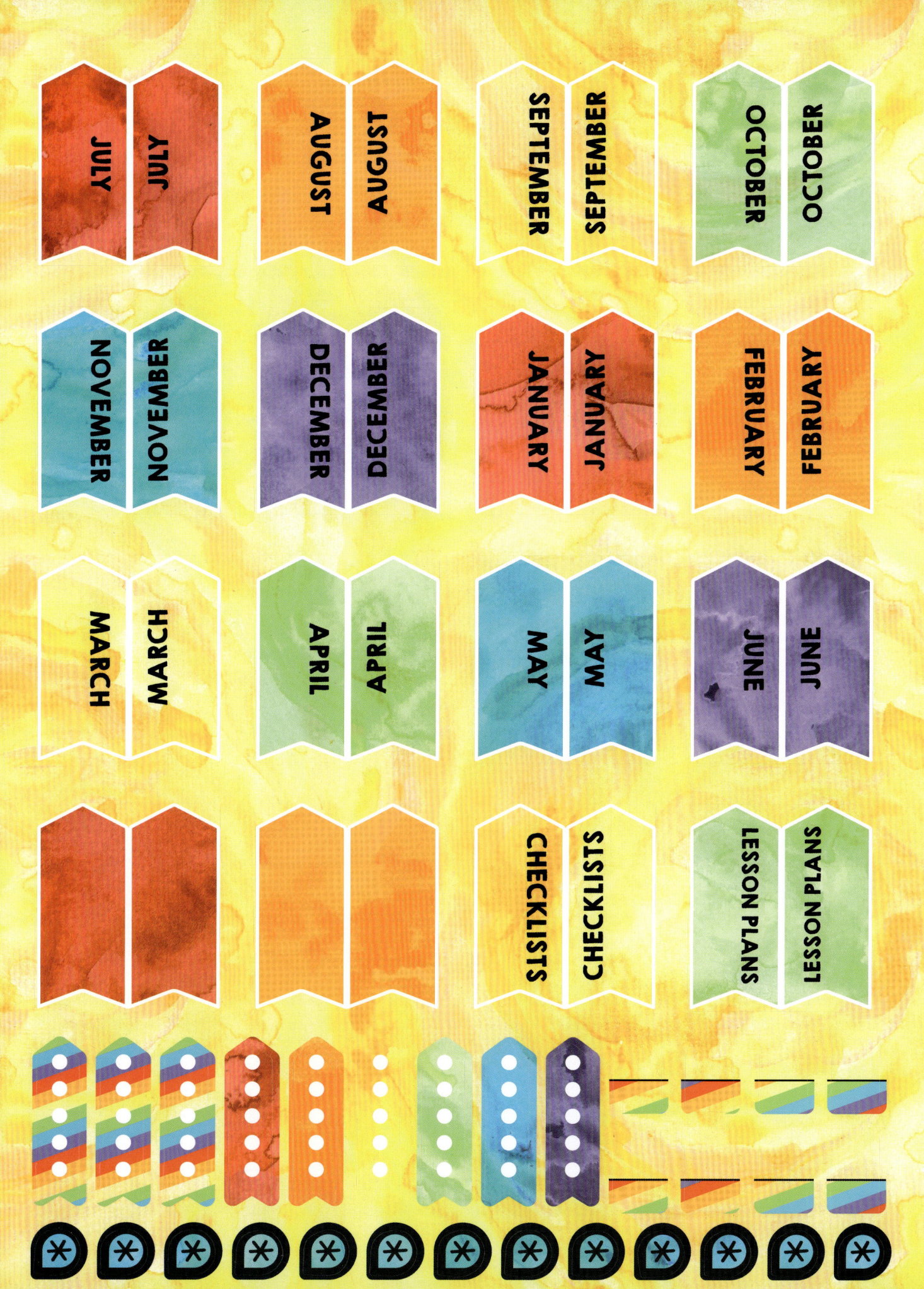